Lots of people dressed
up for fun,

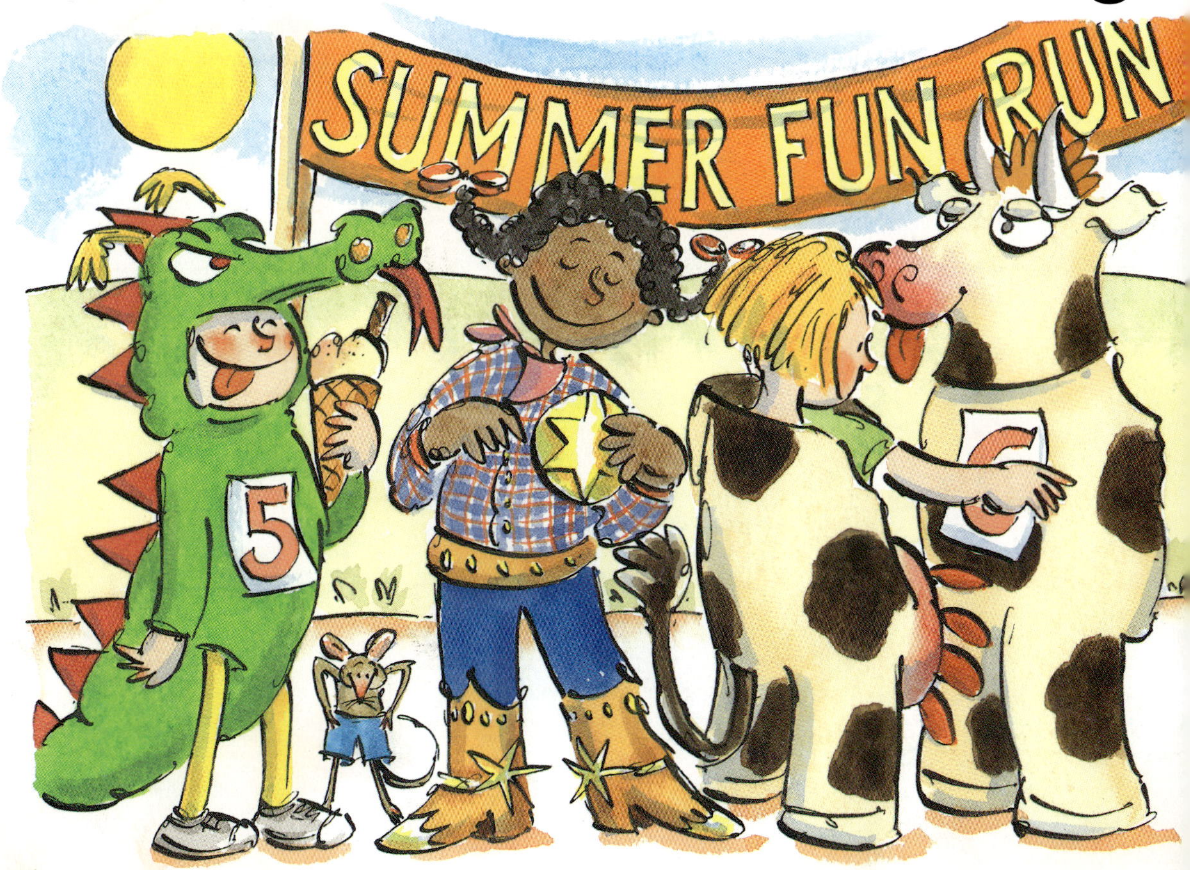

1

a cowgirl, a dragon,
a cow and a sun.

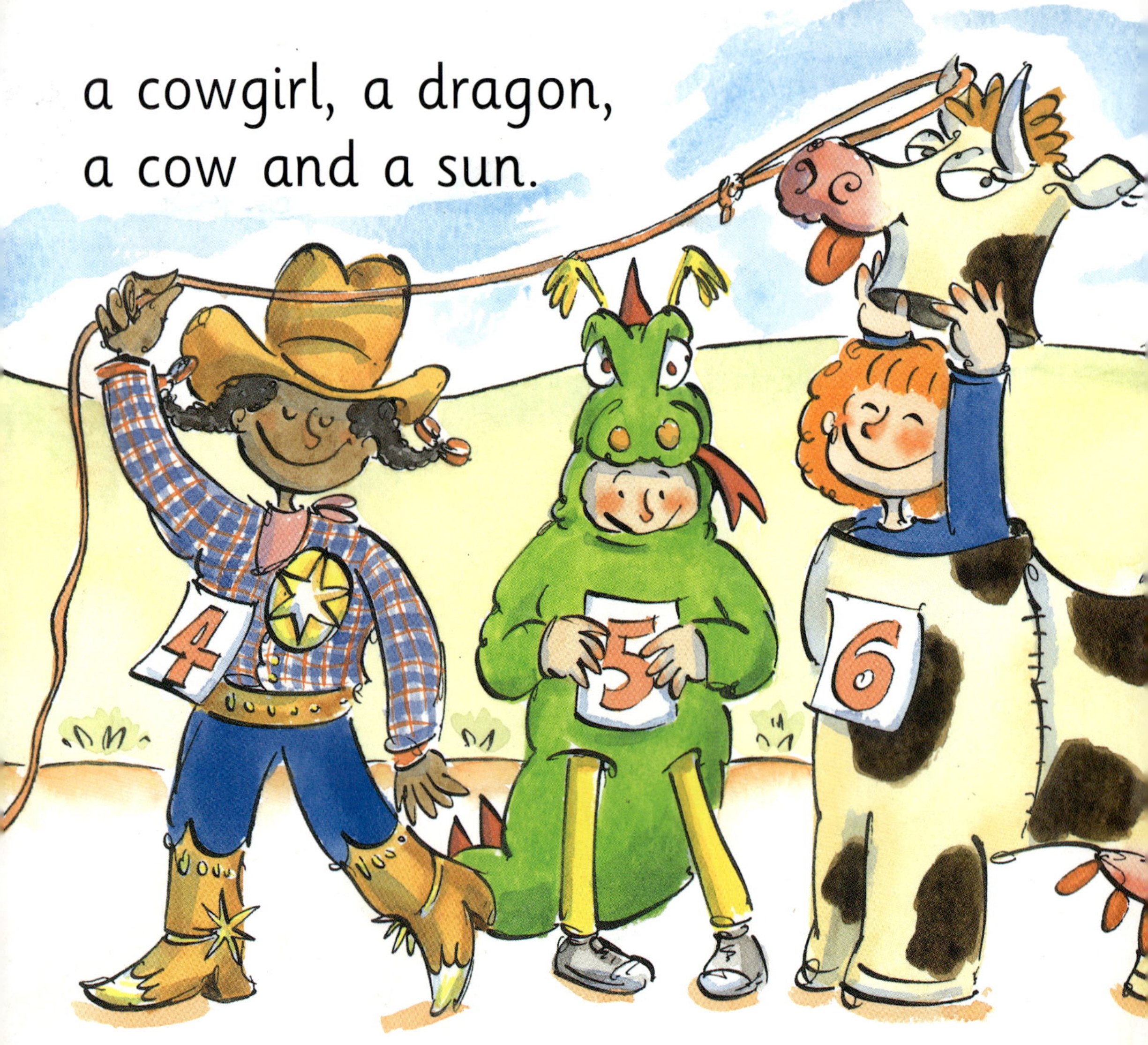

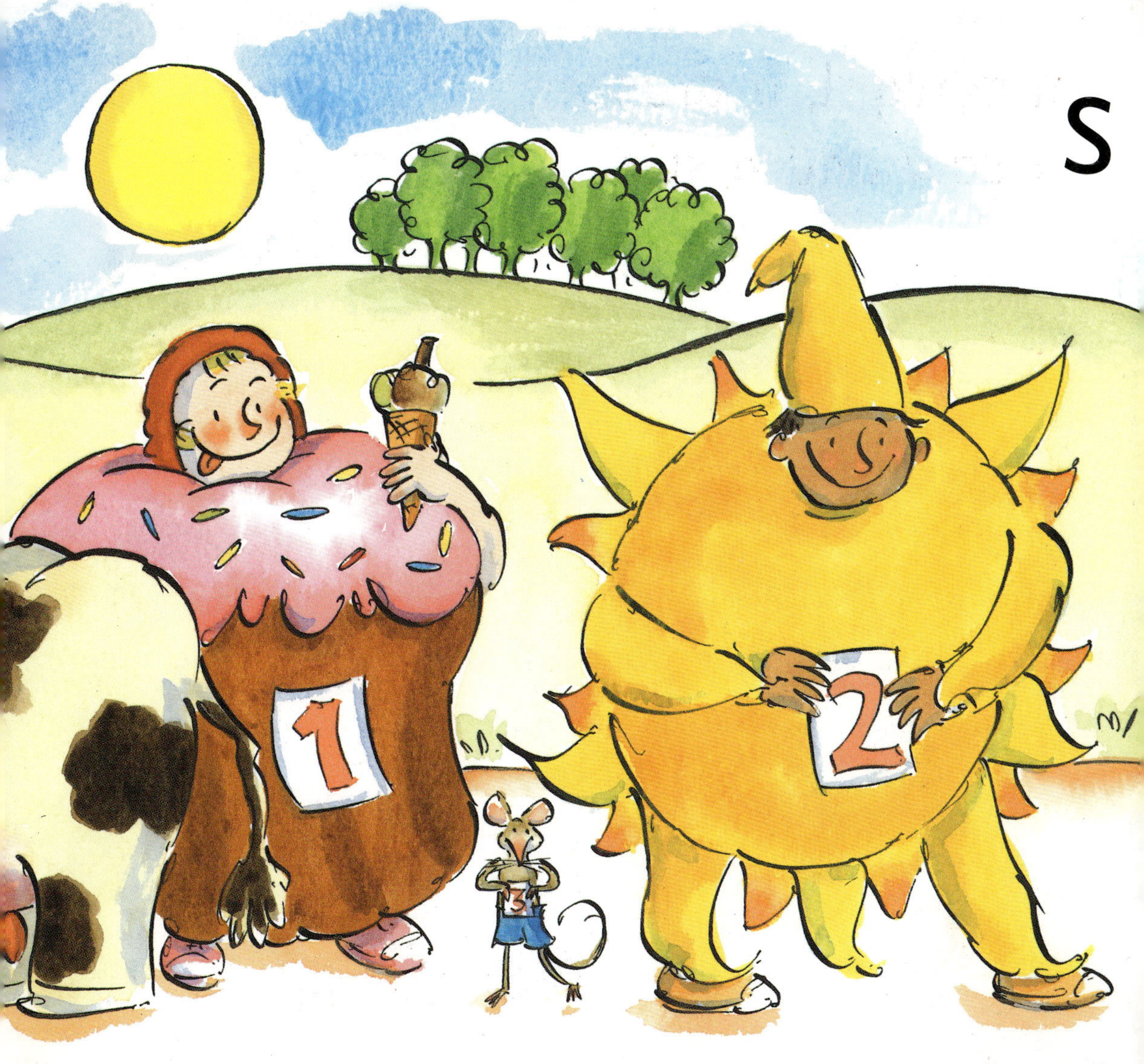
1
2

Get ready, get steady,
they're off at a run!

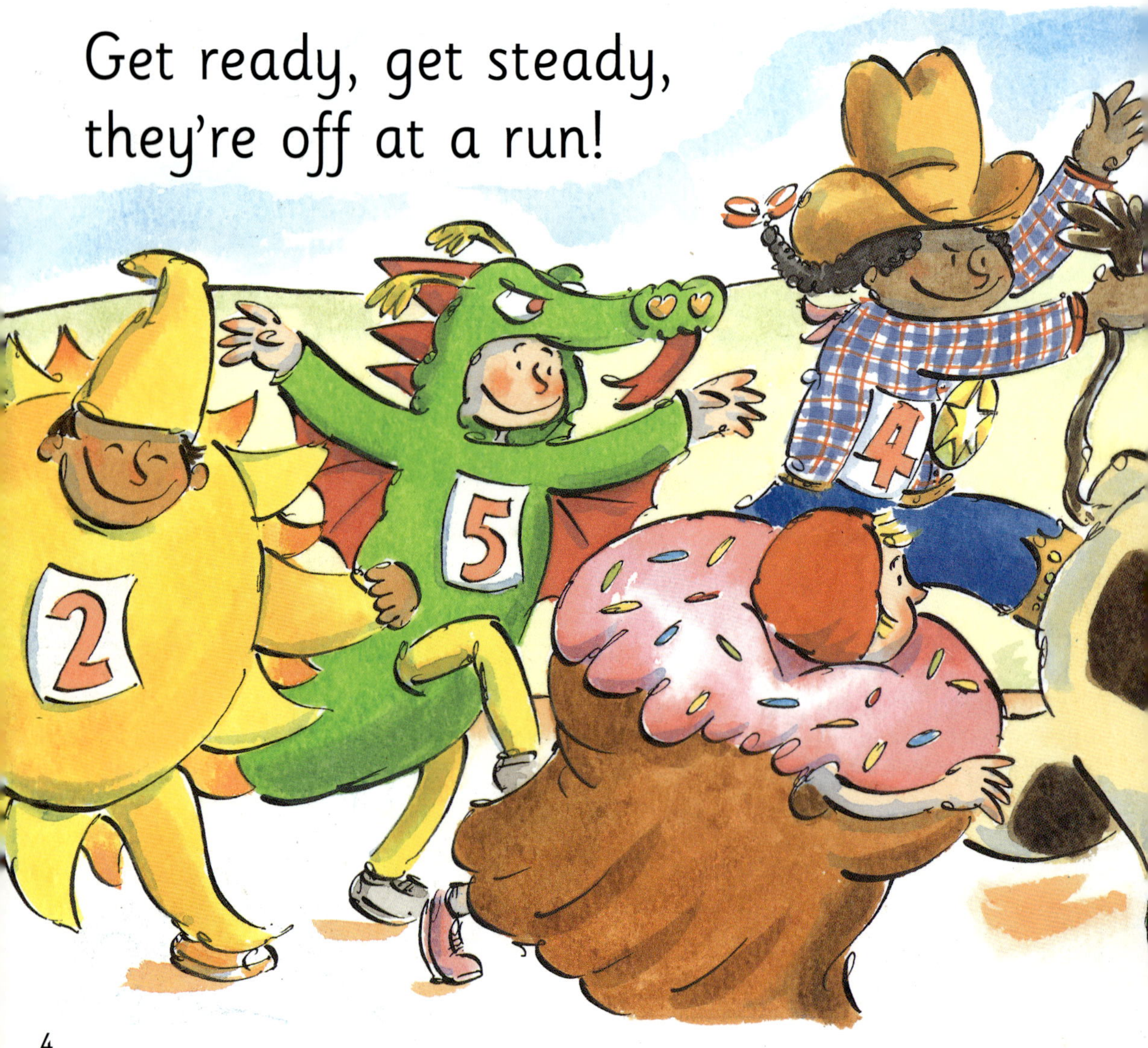

4

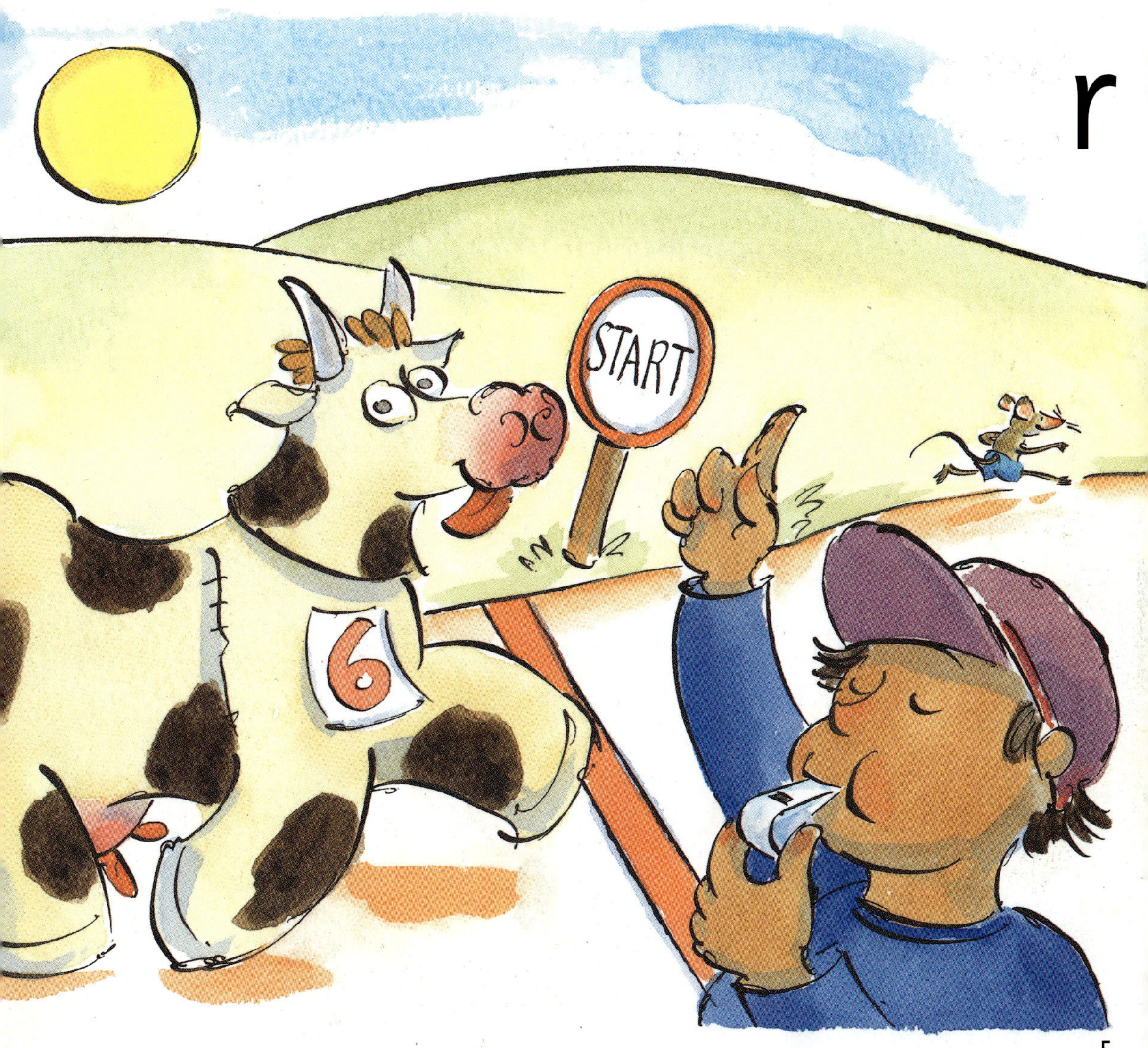
r
START
6

But the cow and the cowgirl
trip over the bun.

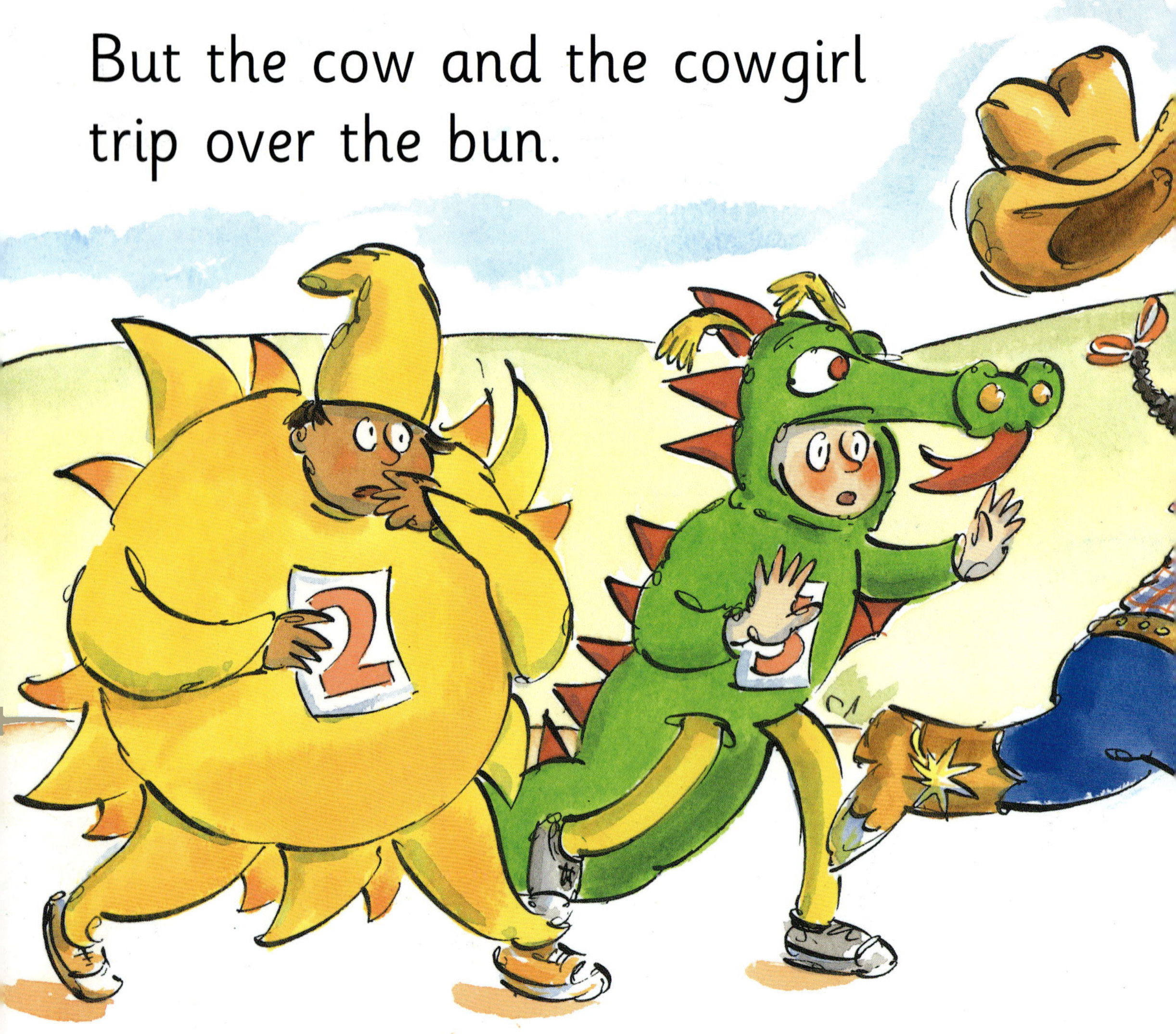

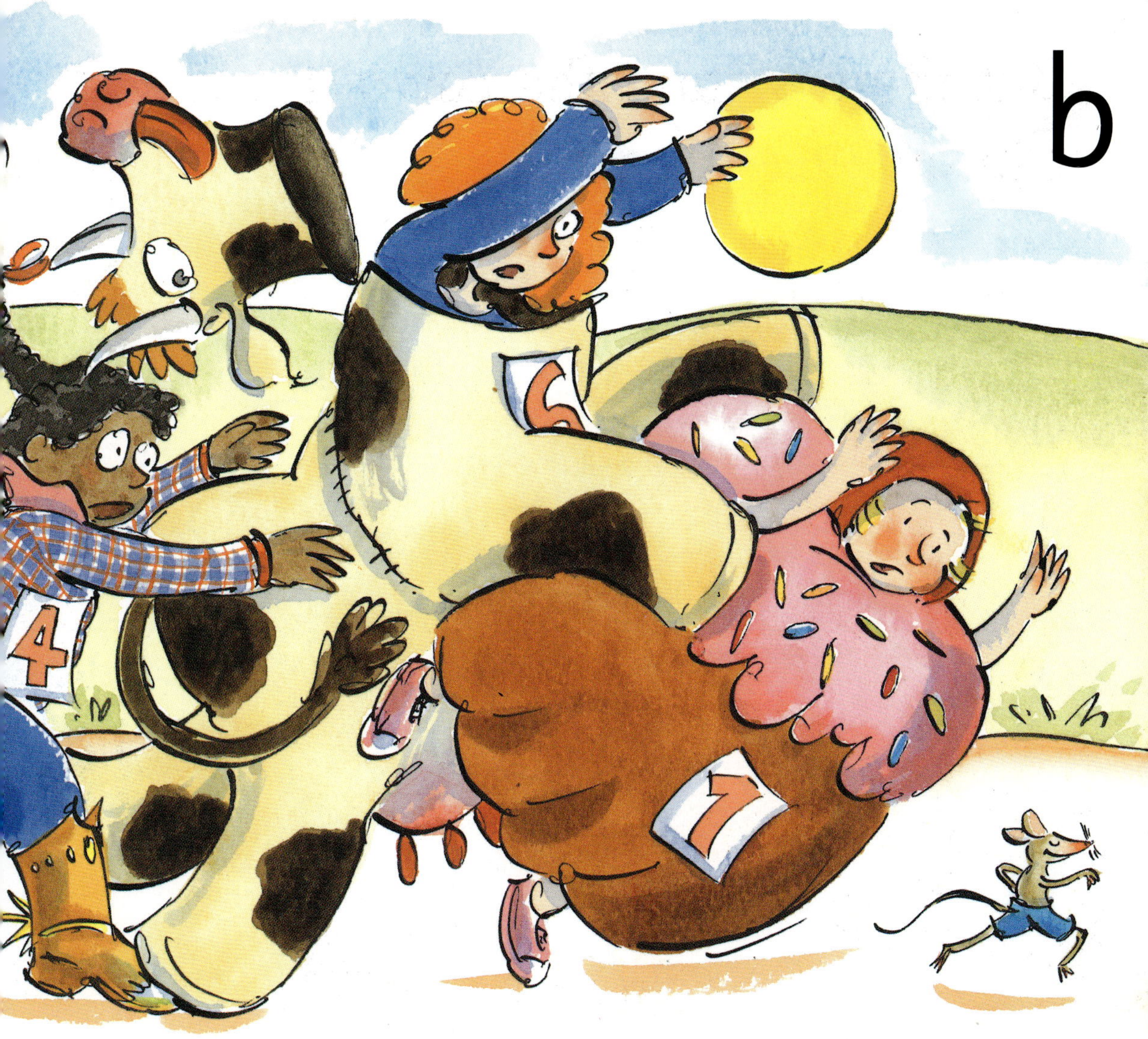
b

And that is the end of
the summer fun run!

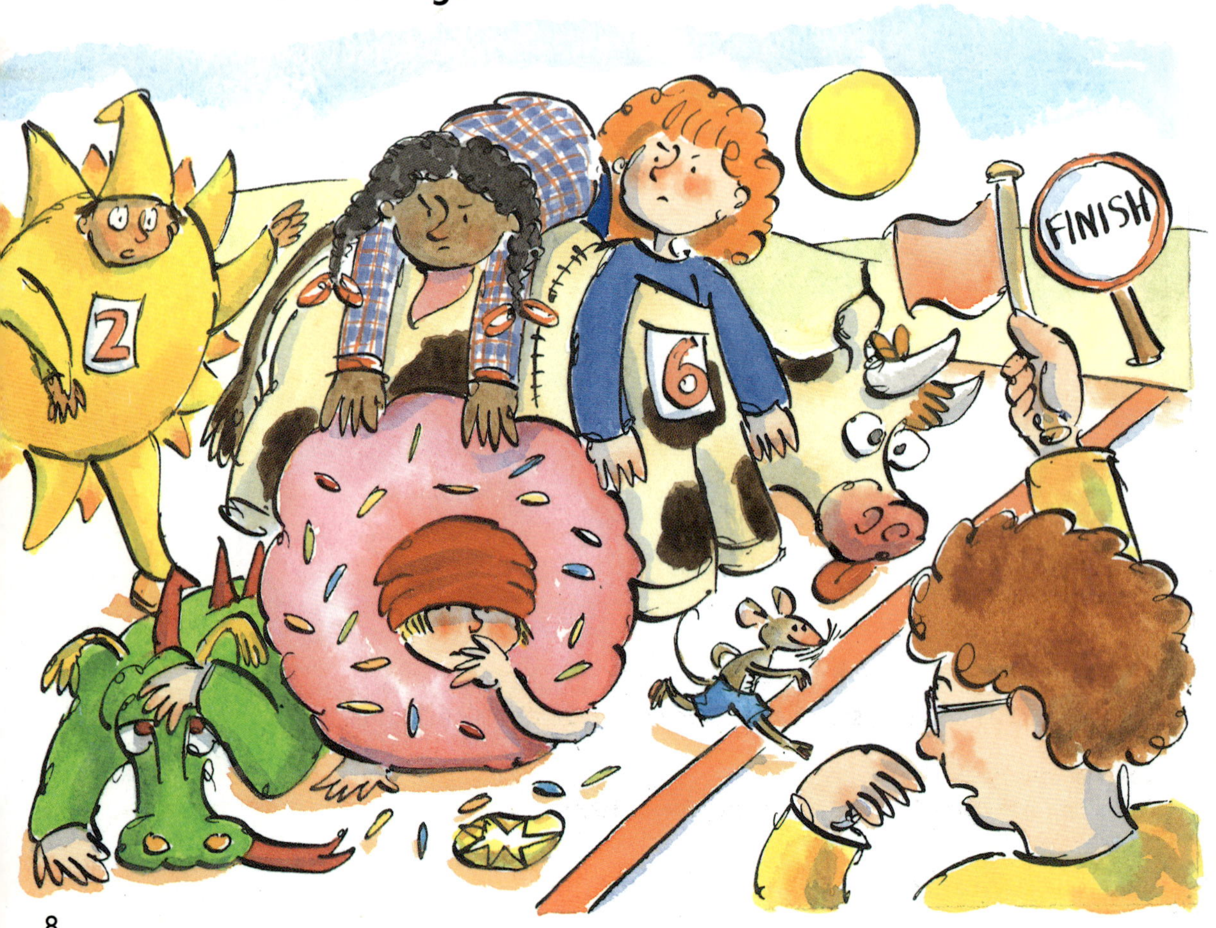